The

LOSER'S
SEMINAR

Traits you must avoid in order
to become wildly successful.

By Saidi Mdala

Published by: GameChangers (Pty) Ltd
Gaborone , Botswana
Cell: +267 76 152 188
Email: saidi@fpb.co.bw

Proofread by Kutlwano Tina Mosime, Tel: +267 393 5796
Layout design by: Evirtek (Pty) Ltd, Cell:+267 73419432
www.evirtek.com | email: frank@evirtek.com

First Edition

ISBN:978-99968-0-283-6

Acknowledgments

This book would not have been possible without the insight, assistance, inspiration and encouragement of these very awesome people.

Mabu Nteta, for advising me to go and write the story of my life in more detail. Jim Rohn for challenging a loser to give a seminar. My extremely supportive protégé, Millicent Kaswada who assured me it had to be done and never stopped pushing me to have it done; Ngwatshi Enyatseng – who read the very first draft and assured me she would buy the first copy if I ever published the book; Julia Chigwende, who offered to review my book if I ever got around to writing one – she did and she pushed that I publish it too!

My good friend Selwana Pilatwe-Koppenhaver who, after reviewing the manuscript, made me realize this book was greater than I thought. To Dr Didi Biorn, you – my sister – administered the last push.

Dr. Marie-Paule Donsimoni-Bupp who said to me; "Kid, you have an amazing way of giving perspective to reality."

Obert Chakarisa, Mike Mudimu, Joy Setshedi, Farah Gray and all those whose stories it was difficult to leave out of this book; and to all the great writers and thinkers whose wisdom I constantly borrowed from – I record my sincerest appreciation.

And Tina Mosime, thanks so much for finally agreeing to proofread **a** soft copy!

Lastly I want to acknowledge God's never failing answer to my simple prayer every time I set out to start writing or speaking in public:

"The Good Lord, please guide my pen and speak through me always."

Dedication

Firstly, this book is dedicated to three permanently special *girls* in my life, Mirriam Jameela & Asiyatu Thandolwenkosi – my two lovely daughters who have reposed amazing faith in me since day one; and Asiyatu Mdala senior – my dear mother, who spared no effort in making sure I made it in life.

Secondly, I dedicate this book to the two greatest men in my life, my late son Abdullah Beverly Mdala and his late grandfather, my father, mentor and the wisest man I have ever spent time with, Jannat Abdalla Mdala – he gave me the greatest gift of life ever – the culture of reading.

Lastly, but certainly not least, to all my friends (including those who faithfully follow me on Facebook) and sympathisers who kept reminding me that writing was my primary benefit, especially Webster Muonwa.

CONTENTS

Why A Loser's Book?

This book you are reading right now is the only such book in the world. And it might just be the one thing that will help change your fortunes or those of someone you know. It is a book written by me, once a celebrated loser, to warn others about the useless traits that make it impossible for many to lead worthwhile lives or achieve success in many of life's pursuits.

Hundreds of thousands of books have been written on achieving success and many more continue to be churned out by the day. Amazingly many people read these books, attend seminars and get motivated for a short while before sliding back to their old unproductive ways.

For a long time I have wondered if there could be something wrong with these inspirational and motivational books, or the people who read them.

I have devoured quite an impressive number of these books myself and I can assure you that there is nothing wrong with the books and the wealth of success principles, tips, techniques and even practical examples they contain. I can also tell you that there is absolutely nothing wrong with the person who reads personal development books but remains the same or even deteriorates. I did that for the greater part of my life and never had to see a shrink.

Still something just did not add up. There always seemed to me that there must be some kind of explanation to this mystery. The challenge was that I could not put my finger on it. After much pondering I decided to approach the puzzle differently.

A lot of answers to our challenges can be derived from our own life experiences. So I took a trip back to the day I arrived on this Green Earth and slowly walked back to the present day. Half way through my expedition, it all came crashing down on me like a fifty-storey building.

Jim Rohn once challenged that it would have been very interesting to have a loser give a seminar:

"Tell us how he messed it all up."

"Unfortunately," said the personal development legend, "Losers never get to do so or make it to seminars like these!"

And I dare add; neither do they write books on how they screwed up their lives so that others can learn from their mistakes and avoid walking the same barren path.

"It would be very useful ..." touted Mr Rohn.

Certified - Loser

I started writing this book when I was two months shy of forty. By then a certified loser, I was working for a friend who thought, and treated me as if, I was an idiot. And boy was he right. It was difficult for anyone who pondered a bit about my life to not think so.

I was crowding forty and, despite apparent intelligence, hard work, honesty, a modest education, creative thinking abilities and several other talents, I had virtually nothing to show for being around for four decades.

I had no car, no house or a piece of land to build one on. I had not satisfied my dowry obligations in full for both my previous two marriages from which I was blessed with two fantastic daughters.

I obtained my driver's license 21 years late, at 37! And at 39 I had no bank account; was gainfully employed, but struggling to pay rentals for one small room. I was literally struggling just to get by.

And one more tiny detail: I completed my four year college degree in seven years –18 years after leaving high school.

We call that a classic loser. It is also the reason why my story is important to you; any loser you might want to help, or any young person who wants to grow up knowing what to avoid in life in order to be successful.

I almost came close to writing off my miserable first forty years on this Ever Green Earth as a total waste but decided otherwise. My life's first forty years here were not a complete waste. They could be used as a bad example!

So I resolved to write a book on the most common traits of a loser as they had affected my own prospects of success one too many times in a life that never stopped going in circles for as long as I can remember.

My argument was very simple. In a world where over 96% of the people in any given social setting are either mediocre or outright losers; preaching about success alone is quite tricky. The reason is equally simple; losers identify more with failure than they do with success. Well-meaning people will always encourage you:

"Yes, you can have anything you want in life. All you have to do, like I did, is have a success mentality. Always think success. Fake it until you make it!"

What do you think is the impact of these words of encouragement to a school leaver who has failed her secondary school certificate, gone in circles for three years without getting a job, is pregnant, barefooted, hungry and hopeless? Of course, the motivational statement is great, except the poor, perhaps, despondent girl will not identify with it.

True. People, especially the distressed, want to hear elevating stuff about how insanely successful they can become in life. But that would make sense as icing on the cake. Success motivation being the icing and the challenges people grapple with – with which they can easily identify and, perhaps, what caused them – being the cake.

Why do you think Mark Victor Hansen and Jack Canfield's Chicken Soup for the Soul and the rest of that incredibly amazing series made such a hit worldwide and continue to inspire action in the lives of the different readers who come across it? Simple! Chicken Soup stories are real life accounts that highlight challenges first, before they tell you of how the affected people dealt with their unfortunate situations and went on to become successful.

In other words, they make the ground fertile first by using some unfortunate story or tragedy that people can identify with before saying: "If Joe could overcome this, you sure can, if you can put your mind to it!"

I wrote this book to help others by highlighting all the stupid decisions I made and some idiotic habits I developed during the first 40 years of my life. If you can avoid half these blunders, you are guaranteed to end up wildly successful. And believe me, you want to know how I threw opportunities away and made bizarre decisions that cost me dearly and still did nothing about it until I had flushed 40 years of a life time down the toilet.

One more thing! You, or someone who matters to you, do not have to go down the same wretched road I trudged. If you can recognize pitfalls in advance, you can avoid them. That is why I decided to write this book. And that is why it is important for you to read it.

And if it works for you, be thankful to Jim Rohn who challenged a loser to give a seminar and show others exactly what NOT to do. And pat yourself on the back for making the decision to read beyond this point.

A What-Not-To-Do Self Help Book

So, for a change, enjoy reading a what-NOT-to-do self-help book that emphasizes what you should avoid as you navigate the ever tricky and often precarious terrain of life. If you can relate to my mistakes, you can challenge the way you have done things up to now and change accordingly.

Maxwell Maltz said: "If you can challenge it you can unlearn it."

And if you can unlearn anything you can re-learn, in its place, something useful.

We call that education and it often happens after school!

Meanwhile you might be successful, or you might have messed your life up, big time, and probably think you do not need this book. But I can bet my worthless first forty years that you still need this book for your child, sibling, friend, colleague, or anyone, for that matter, who you think can benefit from avoiding the road I travelled: a road travelled by many losers who have walked this world before me. These people make up more than 96% of the population of any society, at any given time! Shocking? Yes. True? Absolutely!

Let's get it on with it.

Chapter 1

A loser will sacrifice all opportunity for school

Stay in school

*Create opportunities while you are in school –
try out things*

Get an education

And if something works out, go for it!

Don't sacrifice opportunity for school

This I did for the bulk of my first forty years on this Ever Green Earth, with the same result. It is perhaps the biggest undoing for what would have been my ticket to success well before age 15! And I started early in life too.

I bought and used the wrong life philosophy; the losers' philosophy, not once, but too many times than I care to remember. The sad thing is that a lot us do it so frequently that it becomes a way of life. Why do you think the earth is populated by more than 96% losers?

Let us get something right before we go very far. You go to school so that you get an education and use it to create opportunities: for making money, getting rich or just leading a fulfilling life. So while you are in school, if an opportunity presents itself, the wisest thing to do is to grab it and run with it, even if it means dropping out of school to do so. Education is not found inside the four walls of the classroom only. In fact most of it is found outside the silos we call school. And hey, for the record, school is good and necessary. It just is not indispensable.

Take it this way. You want to grow vegetables in your backyard for sale and make some money. While digging in the garden you discover some diamond deposits in the same place. Do you ignore the diamonds and continue with your gardening or do you abandon the gardening and shift your focus to the newly found mine?

You are probably smiling and saying: "Silly, the answer is obvious." Well, most of the time the answer is not so obvious, especially if gardening is equivalent to attending school and the diamonds to a business opportunity.

If they have to make a choice, losers often choose to stick to the original idea and let opportunities met on the way wash down the drain. That is why everybody is busy with gardening!

I talk to a lot of brilliant young people who I think should be out there making things happen, but are stuck in school. Often they tell me they cannot. I ask; "Why not!"

"Because I am still in school," or "I have to finish school first," are the common answers I get.

This is a useless way of thinking, and I have my life to prove that.

Eight years old and foolish

I was 8 years old when I climbed on to the losers' train from which I never once stepped down for the following 32 years. Some might argue that at 8 a person is only a child and does not have the wisdom to tell what is, and what a lifetime break is not. I have news for you.

Every human being learns 85% of everything, all the information, he or she uses throughout life before reaching age eight. Translation: you have 85% wisdom to use for deciding what you want to do for the rest of your life by age seven.

W Clement Stone started his sales career at six, selling newspapers, and went on to build a multi-billion dollar business later in life.

Billionaire and Google co-founder, Larry Page might sound more familiar for those not privileged with the reading culture and do not know Mr. Stone.

Page started taking machines apart before age eight and by twelve he had made up his mind that he was going to invent things and eventually start a company. Man, am I not happy that he did.

And if you are still not familiar with both Stone and Page you must sure know, whatever your religious persuasion, about a young boy who lived a little over 2000 years ago in the Middle East. His name was Jesus. By age six, Jesus, had made up his mind what he was going to do for a living and was already giving sermons in his *father's* house to grownups who wondered who this whiz kid was.

But if that too is not familiar, then Jaden Smith, an American child actor, will surely ring a bell. He took his first acting role in the inspirational movie, *The*

Pursuit of Happyness at age 8 and went on to belt out a few more movies.

When I was writing this book his CV had grown to include rap music, songwriting and dancing. And believe you me it had very little to do with him being Will Smith's son.

But my all-time favourite is an entrepreneur called Dr Farrah Gray, an African American young man raised by a single mother in the Chicago Project. He was 21 years old when I wrote this book.

Farrah sold body lotion door to door for a dollar-fifty at age six. At age seven he carried a business card that read, *21st Century CEO*; and at age eight co-founded the Urban Neighbourhood Economic Enterprise Club. At nine, Gray reached 12 million listeners and viewers every Saturday night as co-host of "*Backstage Live*," a syndicated television and radio simulcast (simultaneous broadcast) in Las Vegas.

At age twelve, Farrah had a lucrative career with speaking engagements which earned him between five and ten thousand dollars per appearance. At age thirteen he started Farr-Out Foods which he sold at age fourteen for a million dollars – becoming a millionaire at that age!

At sixteen, Farrah acquired an inner city magazine and at seventeen financed a comedy show on the Las Vegas Strip.

Farrah became the youngest member of the Board of Advisors for the Las Vegas Chamber of Commerce. Meanwhile, at the age of fifteen, he was also given a three-year term on the Board of Directors of United Way of Southern Nevada and continued his philanthropic work signing on as the spokesman for the National Coalition for the Homeless and the National Marrow Donor Program.

As a private consultant, he has worked with the likes of JP Morgan Chase and the U.S. Department of Commerce Minority Development Agency.

Farrah has authored three successful books, *"Reallionaire,"* *"Get Real, Get Rich"* and *"The Truth Shall Make You Rich."*

He received an honorary doctorate (Humane Letters) from Allen University.

What more? Dr. Gray is the youngest person to have an office in Wall Street.

Quite breathtaking! Good. Now I think we are on the same page!

The point I am trying to make is that Farrah Gray started at age six!

At eight I started my first business as a manufacturer. After saving some change I got from my parents and some few visitors who took a liking to my sweet character and wit, I invested into a kilogram of brown sugar and a pint of milk. I stole one of my mother's treasured big black pots and made my first batch of sweets. We used to call them fudges (don't ask me why – I was too focused on making money to find out then).

The following day at break time, I did not go playing with others as usual. Instead, I stood by some convenient point in the school grounds and sold my product which was a bit over baked but tasted sweet and looked irresistible to the small sweet-tooth customers who gladly parted with their half cents for each.

A month later, I was having running battles with my mother for messing up her favourite pots and the demand for my products was rising. I realised that manufacturing was taking a toll on me and decided to diversify into retailing. After an inquiry with a local wholesaler, I discovered that I could buy pockets of assorted ready made and neatly wrapped sweets from different manufacturers and resell them at an even greater profit than I made from my home *factory* venture.

I wasted no time in switching and every Wednesday and Friday (when there were no afternoon lessons) I walked a distance of almost eight kilometers to and from town to make my orders with fellow business*men*, most of them much older than me but very supportive and protective.

I made very good money which I deposited in a homemade wooden bank and when it could no longer hold, re-deposited the money with mother – a very trustworthy and secure banker. By my second year in business I was so smart I could count money and make a few smart business decisions: like employing my young sister and cousin to sell some of the sweets for me. On commission!

I was in third grade when I made the first of what became a series of blunders in my life.

At one point school began interfering with business. My parents believed in school than they did in business. I gave in to parent pressure and ditched business. This was despite the fact that I could count better than anyone else and read more than any of my grade mates.

I counted hundreds of sweets and coins every week and invested in comic books that I voraciously consumed during the time I was neither in school nor selling my sweets outside the sports stadium.

But I threw it all away because I bought the wrong life philosophy and sacrificed my business for school. This was despite the fact that I could have done both or, better still, ditched school and pursued business and *education* instead. Yes that's right, education, for that is what I was getting doing business.

As a young business person, I got to practically do some accounting and wages too! Every evening I did some reconciliation with my sister and cousin and paid their commissions. And the reason I ever made any profit was because I had learnt about smaller margins and quick returns and used that trick to outsell my competition.

I was enjoying life as a business*man*, and it was great and fun indeed.

Hey I was smart. What nine year-old invests in comic books to improve reading proficiency and creativity in writing?

So why did I let it all go? Simple.

Somewhere along the way I bought and succumbed to a bad philosophy – a dangerously limiting philosophy for any young person. It said: "Either you take school or you take school."

Translation: young boys like me had no business selling sweets at break time or outside stadiums during the weekends. They were supposed to be doing school homework or just being kids.

School, as the system promised, would guarantee me a good job and a decent wage. I was to learn later that j.o.b. stands for 'just over broke' and took the privilege to redefine w.a.g.e. to 'wretched, abject, grovelling entity.' Translation: desperate for life and groaning under the merciless yoke of financial dependency.

Unless you are working for Warren Buffet, Microsoft, Apple or Google, being employed by someone else is often a very subhuman ill-informed decision. And even if you are working for any of those great companies, one of the greatest business leaders in corporate America, Jack Welch strongly holds that lifetime employment is a failed strategy.

"So what?" you might say. "You were only a small boy under social pressure and had no option and growing up in then Rhodesia (I did my first two primary school years in pre-independent Zimbabwe) you probably had no exposure to the world or had no hero figure to inspire you."

Moreover, both parents and teachers were inclined to use the notorious corporal punishment when they thought a child had challenges understanding such simple but *useful* concepts as: 'counting bottle tops on the abacus at school is more important than counting coins at the end of every day.'

I wish this could make me feel better for being stupid back then. Far from it.

Number one, I always had an option. Everyone always has an option and we start exercising this privilege as early as one week old small toys in our mothers' laps. Remember when you wanted someone to just hold you and you hollered above your small shrill irritating voice until someone gave in and rocked you to be quiet?

Or when you first backhanded a spoonful of baby porridge insisting you needed milk instead and you ended up getting your way. Or a few years later when you did not like the small outfit they bought without your approval and you rolled over in dirt because you hated it.

I have been raising two smart girls in the 'no-corporal application era' and I remember tens of these incidents very well. They always have options and they exploit them. So did I. Except I always screwed my options up.

I had options and I had one of the most powerful heroes contemporary history has ever recorded: Muhammad Ali, the greatest American heavy weight boxing champion and one of Arnold Schwarzenegger's heroes too. I won all my brawls in primary school imitating his stubbornness. If only I had used the same tenacity to continue with business despite society's silly dictates.

I knew a few boys who had earned a notorious reputation for following their will until their parents and teachers gave up on them. Looking back, I am confident I was way smarter than them.

But I was a loser. I bowed down to pressure; and that is what makes a loser. S/he abandons what works now for some distant false promise – like a college diploma or degree and a good job. Later in life I got both of the first two but never the third one.

All the people I saw around going through the drab school process then, later worked as teachers, nurses or bank tellers. Most remained mediocre. Today, many years later, the trend is the same.

In fact it has become worse. Back then you had to fail your secondary school certificate to be unemployable in any of the available decent jobs. Nowadays you have to go as far as university to achieve the same and you have to pass with great grades too!

Again, I am not saying do not go to school or university, I am simply saying – when the opportunity comes about – try out your hand at making money or doing something you really enjoy while you go to school. Or better yet, use school days to proactively try different entrepreneurial ideas. You have the time, some change and a lot of energy to do so. And you can be having a blast while at it. Mark Zuckerburg created Facebook in a dorm room while boozing.

And when, at any point, you hit jackpot throw everything down and do what you have to. We go to school so that we can earn a living. And when we discover a way to earn a living earlier then there is no need to stay a second further in school.

And mind you, it is not about money. Life has a lot more useful pursuits through which you can craft for yourself a fulfilling existence. But you will always find that money is very much a significant facilitator in all of those pursuits. When you get a chance to make money, step out of the zoo and get on with it.

Speaking of the zoo, a very interesting story is told about a teenage camel and her mother in a zoo.

Asked the smart young camel:

"Mother why are we even-toed?"

Mother camel: So that our hooves support our weight evenly and we do not sink in the sand.

Young Camel: And the humps on our back?

Mother camel: They are fatty deposits which help us muster more energy in hot situations.

Young camel: And the funny nostrils?

Mother camel: (impatient) They are not funny, they are designed to limit water loss, and our thick coats are for reflecting sunlight, and insulation from the intense heat radiated from desert sand.

Our long legs help by keeping us farther from the hot ground while our mouths are very powerful, to enable us to chew thorny desert plants.

The long eyelashes and ear hairs, together with sealable nostrils, form a barrier against sand.

(Mother camel heaved a sigh before challenging her amazed young one)

Mother Camel: Satisfied?

Young camel: Not exactly mother, why do we need all these special features?

Mother camel: Stupid question – so that we can survive in the dessert.

Young camel: (now with a baffled and worried look): So what are we still doing in a zoo?

Moral of the story: yes you guessed right. Once you have developed the right faculties, skills and techniques, never stay a day longer in the zoo. It is very easy to get used to useless habits.

And guess what?

Being stupid can become a habit

During my second year in college, I was offered a lucrative job opportunity at a reputable mine and turned it down preferring to finish the academic year instead. I was on my way to becoming a serial loser.

Later when I was working on my college degree

I attended an interview with a foreign based Insurance Agent whose director thought I would make it big time in his company. Back home I thought about abandoning my part-time schooling and started developing cold feet. Eventually I let the opening go gaping.

Even after discovering that I could transfer my credits to an institution in another country and finish my studies there, I still found some straw to clutch at and floated to the next empty island. Another lost opportunity.

I was over thirty and there was every indication that the disease was now chronic. You do not learn anything the second time you are kicked by a mule.

It is insanely amazing how school served to keep me away from opportunities all my life. Or more precisely, how I used school as a smoke screen for not grabbing many golden opportunities that I let slip through my fingers like sand in an hourglass.

My advice to you – the wisdom of a loser: Never let that happen to your precious life. And I am not at all saying, do not go to school. Stay in school. Just do not stick there a minute longer when a life opportunity comes along.

And now a few lessons to take home:

School is important. So go to school and as far as necessary, stay in school. But when an opportunity to make money or start a lifetime career presents itself and you are forced to choose between the two, ditch school and go for the opening.

School is supposed to help create opportunities for you later in life and to a lesser extent, give you some useful education. So when an opportunity comes earlier – and they often do – grab it and ruthlessly pursue it. And if school stands in the way, well, run it over.

Of course that is not bad advice; neither am I bad influence to school going youth or even adults. School is only necessary before you discover your big break in life, and when you do, it is time to leave the zoo and learn while on the field.

Meanwhile I have a few examples of people who did the right thing when confronted with a situation that demanded making a choice between school and a life's career.

Thomas Edison the great inventor attended school up to third grade before engaging in what mattered most in his life – a career of inventions. Thanks to him we can read and socialize at night under the light bulb – one of his many inventions.

Henry Ford had no education worth writing home about but he used his opportunity when it came to change the course of history by inventing the self-propelled modern automobile, the Ford T-Model.

Abraham Lincoln, the man who became one of the most illustrious United States presidents and abolished slavery, only attended formal school for 12 months. Still he became a lawyer at 32 because he knew exactly what he wanted to get out of life, with or without going to school.

Billionaire and philanthropist Laurence Graff has phenomenal interest in improving the lot of the African child, and has gone on to invest a lot in infrastructure and modern technologies in rural settings. Graff is chairman of the Graff Diamonds Holdings, a world renowned diamond polishing business and founder of *For Africa's Children Every Time* (FACET).

Laurence left school at 15 to pursue his career in diamonds. Despite a lot of disappointments along the way, he never looked back.

And there is one trailblazing entrepreneur I

once met - Joy Setshedi, then popularly known as Joy Simakane. Joy abandoned school after failing her junior certificate to pursue her dream of becoming a businesswoman. When I first interviewed her, she was the owner and chief executive officer of a global courier company with offices in the United Kingdom, China, Zimbabwe, South Africa and the head office back home in Botswana.

Our second interview was just after she had come back from Switzerland, where she had received the UNCTAD global Empretec Women in Business Award for placing third position.

All these people, and many others, learnt a lot more embracing opportunities that came their way and never listened to any dissenting voice or bowed down to any pressure. All of them had to abandon school as soon as opportunity beckoned.

Of course, I agree, it is not an easy thing to do but then as I said earlier, that is part of the reason why the world is peopled by more than 96% losers.

You choose to be part of the plus 96% losers or the 3%, or so, that defies odds to do what you have to do. But it just does not happen that easily. And that takes us to my second mistake.

Chapter 2

Losers always give in to external pressure

Follow your passion

Never let anybody tell you: You are too young or too old to try something extraordinary

Do not give in to external pressure

Especially parent, family, teacher or social pressure!

After abandoning my business career at nine, I turned all my focus toward school and learnt all sorts of stuff I would never use later in life – like Pythagoras theorem. After that I never once sold anything until much later when I became an insurance salesman and threw that away too, few feet from the gold belt.

In my later primary school years I took a serious liking to music, dancing and building cars. Yes that was not a typographic error – music and building cars!

I threw myself into it. I built a makeshift band from used cooking oil tins, strapped with plastic paper for the drums. Every day after school I would assemble my band instruments and start belting out some original tracks in between popular hits of that moment. I think I had it in my blood as a musician because it attracted a good number of fans from the neighborhood who always came to listen to me play. Some even danced to the music.

For some weird reason every career initiative I made got me into big trouble with my mother and she always had good reasons lined up.

For the band I had all odds stacked against me. First my venue was a disaster. It was right in the middle of my mother's vegetable garden and the audience often left the backyard a mess. Secondly, practice clashed with chores and homework time and, at the same time, competed with mother's beckoning.

After failed attempts by mother, characterized by constant beatings and burning of my band to end my second career; she enlisted father's help. My father was a reverend and band music was categorically a NO-NO in his religious philosophy.

Pressure was brought to bear and I bowed out of music, especially after the night I jumped on stage during a music concert by a popular musician, did my moves and walked away $5 richer. Now that was a lot of money, it cost 15 cents to get a ticket for the show and 5 cents to watch a movie in those days. A two minute dance and I was $5 rich.

The following morning my father got wind of my adventure and after a clash with him, I allowed that too, to slip. Believe you me; you never wanted to get a beating administered by my father.

The same thing happened to the next adventure I tried; making cars. I made great models of toy cars using scrap wire and empty fuel seals. I even used one of my trucks to carry some groceries whenever mother sent me to the shops, and of course got a hiding every time milk pockets got pricked by loose wires or when fresh vegetables fell off my speeding car.

Each time this happened mother punctuated the beating by smashing the vehicles and after a while I got frustrated and gave up on that too. Life was getting more and more horrible as an entrepreneur and school seemed to be the only safe thing do.

Little did I know then that safe is not a good option in life. If you want to pick roses be prepared to deal with thorns and in life everything worth achieving is protected by thorns.

Success is not for the irresolute or faint hearted. You know you are on to something big or worthwhile when everybody thinks you are too young or too old to do it, or tell you it cannot be done. You must be prepared to be pricked first to pick a rose or get stung in order to access a honey comb.

And if you give in for the second time there is no guarantee you will ever stand up to the next challenge. I gave up – not twice but many times. I turned into what you may call a serial quitter.

During my last year in primary school I tried making hunting weapons – okay, catapults with slight modifications – for shooting birds, but that was my most short-lived adventure. The beating I received was more severe and the threats even more overwhelming. Shortly afterward, an attempt to create fireworks using bicycle spokes and match sticks met the same fate. My career as an inventor was doomed.

My advice to you when faced with the challenges I buckled under: never let anyone tell you, you cannot do anything you love doing most because of how it makes them feel. This is your life we are talking about and if it gets messed up, you can always un-mess it up later, especially if you start young. There is always plenty of time to learn from your mistakes, if you start making them early in life.

But parents are not very easy people to deal with. Especially when they think bearing children is an extraordinary feat and an automatic endorsement for wisdom.

My mother had a favourite question for me whenever we reached an impasse:

"What do you know about life?" and then rub it in with something that really embarrassed me without fail: "You are a small boy who still wets his bed every night!"

For the record, my mother was a great parent; so was my father and both wanted what they thought was best for me. Only they did not know it was not school. Both had not gone beyond second grade in school and wanted to make a difference by making sure we (my siblings and I) took school all the way to becoming some kind of decent professionals.

This is a timeless parenting disease. It is almost incurable and always mutating into a more complicated state with social evolution. Today, most parents have, at least, gone through secondary education but still hold the argument for school that my unschooled parents held back then.

Even those who have gone all the way to graduating with college degrees still hold the same sterile philosophy that school, especially its academic aspect, is the only way forward in life – never mind any pop up opportunities along the way.

It's not their fault – they are thoroughly schooled but hopelessly uneducated about one of the greatest secret to success:

"Never snooze before an opportunity. You can always learn more as you try your hand at different things."

In case you think these are just rumblings of a loser, listen to one of the most influential persons in the 21st Century.

Your time is limited, so don't waste it living

someone else's life. Don't be trapped by dogma - which is living with the results of other people's thinking. Don't let the noise of other's opinions drown out your own inner voice. And most importantly, have the courage to follow your heart and intuition. They somehow already know what you truly want to become. Everything else is secondary. ~ *Steve Jobs.*

But I am also aware that it takes more than sheer tenacity to prevail against parents whose minds are made up about *what is good for you.*

However you can overcome any impediment if you avoid the terrible trait I share with you in the next chapter.

Chapter 3

Losers float through life without a purpose

Find your purpose, learn about and live it

Create a vision for you purpose

Let that vision guide every activity and choice in your life

Don't be a wandering generality. Be a meaningful specific – Zig Ziglar

Remember you are never too old or too young to have a purpose

If there is something that I shamelessly abused while growing up, it was purposelessness. I indulged it for a good 34 years.

It is fact that where there is no vision the people will perish, just as it is no exaggeration that when you are not going anywhere in particular, any road will take you there. No need to even ask for directions.

Roman statesman Lucius Seneca put it even nicely: when a man does not know what harbour he is making for, no wind is the right wind.

Indeed no wind was ever the right one for me while growing up. In fact every wind was ideal for me – going south or north; east or west and most of the times going in circles. It made no difference. I was not headed for any particular port.

This is why I think I was a very helpful person to others all my first 40 years. I fit into virtually anyone's plan and you have no idea how many people took advantage of that.

Take it from a loser: to have NO purpose in life is to be active without being productive and that is no better than doing nothing at all. In fact you do not put any effort into doing nothing.

Why do you think that two people in the same situation today wind up in different stations in life ten, fifteen years later, one doing great things and the other wallowing in poverty? I never had to sweat the answer to that question. I lived it for a good two decades and a few more years.

Ever came across this remark by Frederick Langbridge?

"Two men looked out from prison bars, one saw the mud, the other saw the stars."

My own story illustrates this in a fantastic way.

During my form 3 and 4 I sat in class next to a very interesting and focused young man named Obert Chakarisa. Obert had no girlfriend in school for the two years that I knew him. And no, he was not gay. He had love for his books – but was not a bookworm. He loved playing soccer, which he was extremely good at.

He spoke very little, was always very unassuming and remained inconspicuous in most vain activities or social settings. He qualifies for what might pass for a nerd, except he was a funny guy when he got up to it.

After completing our Ordinary level studies we met briefly once when we were collecting our results which were amazingly identical – 2 A's, 4 B's and 1 C. We went our separate ways and only reestablished contact after 21 years, thanks to the Internet.

Naturally e-mails flew back and forth as we engaged in some catching up and inevitably compared notes.

In two decades since leaving school Obert had gone on to do an apprenticeship as an Aircraft Engineer. After qualifying, he left to work in neighbouring South Africa.

There he worked for a couple of companies as an Aircraft Engineer before joining the Civil Aviation Authority of Africa's biggest economy (RSA) as an Airworthiness Inspector.

Then he was awarded a scholarship by the French Government to study for a Master's Degree in Aircraft Airworthiness, in Toulouse, France for 15 months. Off he flew to France with his wife and two boys and came back with a Master's Degree after the study period.

He rose through the ranks, skipping a few levels in the process, to become a Senior Manager and was later appointed acting general manager: Air Safety Operations and then executive manager: Aircraft Safety.

He enrolled for an MBA and while working on that, landed the post of General Manager: Aircraft Safety – his position at the time of our exchanges.

His explanation for all this:

"God has been good to me. I am having a great career in aviation and also a great family. I am still very humble, but maybe a bit funnier."

Indeed Obert was just being modest. My explanation for his success story is simple. He had decided well in time what he was going to become and knew which winds to raise sails for at any given time. He had what we often call a vision: a particular focus around which successful people create a purpose for existence at any point in their pursuits.

The same could not be said for me. I cruised through life without a vision and purpose, hoping that by some stroke of luck my ship would get to some port worthwhile.

I had a lot of opportunities and basis for endless choices but with no purpose to trap or attract them, they just zapped past me.

For one, the opportunity to go straight into media school and learn journalism was lost. After I got no response for my application for a place to study I just sat back and assumed that was fine. You see when you have no purpose to fulfill, you are never in any hurry. Everything happens when it happens.

Secondly my application for an apprenticeship opportunity to study electronics with Philips Electrical expired while I walked around with the form they had sent me to fill in and return inside four weeks. The form was duly filled in and placed in a stamped envelope ready for posting. Only I decided to post in my shorts' back pocket every morning right up to the expiry date. You see, losers always assume they will get another chance.

The third incident was even more bizarre. Still keen to do something related to information, I applied for a place to study for a course in Library and Information Science. When the polytechnic college invited me for interviews I was ecstatic. No sooner had I arrived at the college than had all the bliss vanished.

"Unfortunately we do not offer the course you applied for and since you have good grades we thought you would be interested in some of the courses available," explained the administrative secretary.

I was not at all interested in any of the other courses they offered. But since I had no particular port in mind any wind was sure to get me there. I took some other course called Secretarial Studies (certainly not legal studies) with the hope to become, God knows better!

This triggered a series of other instances of accepting whatever was handed to me by fate – another disastrous habit of losers I will discuss in chapter four.

Thus for more than twenty years after finishing secondary school and parting with Obert I was still struggling to do virtually anything for myself and my two girls. I was also fast approaching midlife.

I now know very well that had I defined for myself a vision or purpose early in life, I would have even prevailed against my parents and followed my heart in doing any of the things I tried back then until I had hit jackpot. I would not have bowed down to pressure. I would have remained adventurous even later in secondary school or college.

But, if it is any consolation: then you would not

have had the opportunity to read this book.

And while you smile at that, you can as well learn one more positive thing from my streak of terrible blunders in life: It is never too late (or for that matter too early) to determine a purpose for yourself.

At age 34, while working as a receptionist, I attended a corporate culture transformation seminar organized by my employers then. It was facilitated by a cynical but amazingly inspiring transformational expert called Dr. Alex Benjamin Madzivire. It lasted for three days, and left a permanent mark in my life. My purposeless roller coaster life ground to a screeching halt and a new chapter opened. If you ever get anything useful out of this book, you owe it, predominantly, to those three fateful days. They helped me uncover my purpose.

But an even bigger lesson is that you do not have to wait until you are 34 to discover your purpose. You need it earlier in life to determine everything that is going to happen to you: the subjects you will take interest in, in school, the friends you will make, the career you will pursue, the religion you will follow, the person you will choose to marry, the biggest contribution you will voluntarily make to humanity and, most importantly the person you will become in the process – the last part being your vision.

Stephen R Covey stressed that discovering your purpose in life and keeping it alive by relentlessly pursuing it, is the main thing in anyone's life.

"The main thing is to keep the main thing the main thing," he said. I can't agree more.

Chapter 4:

Losers Take Whatever Is Handed Down to Them

Know what you want and why

Learn to say NO! to nonsense

Never compromise your worth for anything

But without a purpose and vision, losers specialize in taking whatever is handed down to them. My incident back in college where I wound up taking a course I had not intended to study is a very good example. And that was just the beginning.

I had always taken what was handed down to me because I had always thought that my choices were limited to what was available. This is an entrenched loser's philosophy.

Often because of this, losers cannot say 'No!'

For some weird reason they assume if they do, they would lose everything – even when there is nothing to lose.

Alexander Hamilton said it better: "Those who stand for nothing fall for anything."

Losers do this for a living and for me it was once second nature. With no purpose of my own, I stood for nothing and anything carried the day.

I am sure you remember my idiotic decision that led me to settle for a course I had not applied for, after being told that this particular college did not offer my desired course. That is not where it all started.

Meanwhile, it is like getting to a bus station and being told there are no buses going to your intended destination, but there is one going in the opposite direction and still has seats. And guess what, you smile and jump on to it!

It started when I was in form three. The school policy was that students who did very well would go into the *sciences* class while those who scored lower would go into the other two classes that specialized in arts subjects. In the place of a subject called Extended

Science (whatever that was), they would study English Literature. I loved literature studies.

I discovered early in life that I was not cut out for anything mathematical and was predominantly a right brain person. I had no business bothering myself with calculations instead of learning to create my own reality using the mystery of language. But I settled for the sciences class. I did not quite know what I would do with the science subjects later in life. I am not sure I have had to take recourse to those studies in any meaningful way up to now.

Then, came, the college incident I related earlier.

Remember the Old Boys' law: You don't learn anything the second time you are kicked by a mule.

After college my third job was with some quasi Non-Governmental Organisation as some administration clerk – whatever that means, again. During the interview I was promised a monthly salary of 2,100.00, of that country's local currency to which I agreed. It was a lot of money then.

A few days later my employment contract came in bearing a monthly salary of 1,200.00. Underpaid. But I thought:

"No that was very clear when we discussed and agreed upon it." There was only one rational explanation. It must have been a typographic error made by a secretary after having bad lunch and inadvertently reversing the first two digits. I immediately pointed this out to the respective authority who emphatically said it was not a typo error.

"That is the correct rate for your post," he stressed and I said OK, much to my own surprise.

I agreed and hung up the phone. I was feeling anything but OK. I seethed with anger inside after dropping the phone. I ranted and raved. Boy was I livid. But after that entire emotional circus, I did nothing more to express my displeasure or appeal for correction. Instead I signed the contract and hamstrung myself to a salary almost half of what I had negotiated initially.

My fear was as stupid as it was baseless: this was the only opportunity I had and could not afford to lose it. That is a typical loser's philosophy, and poor me, one that I held for a good part of my grown up life.

Later I joined an insurance broking company that paid using some funny commission system where sales people always received the shorter end of the stick. I slaved for this company for two years, getting whatever was handed down to me without asking any questions. I am sure by now you know why.

Then came the most banal period of my career – seven years turning up for work every day for eight hours to parrot three to four lines on the company's switchboard. And this is how I landed that job.

I attended the interview for this job together with some younger chap who knew exactly what he wanted and told me he was not going to settle for a penny less than he had in mind. They offered both of us less than we had indicated on the job application forms. My newly found friend snubbed the offer and left. You guessed right: I took it.

Despite the fact that I still had another job I could go back to, I feared if I said 'no' to their offer, I would lose 'everything'. Thus I condemned myself to seven years of the most menial jobs I have ever had to do, even with the contemptible college diploma obtained after two years of study.

Realizing that my two precautious daughters would never understand why a normal grown up man with a college diploma would eventually retire as a receptionist, I decided to enroll for a college degree in psychology.

The distant learning institution I approached told me there was no psychology enrollment for that academic year. My second option was another undergraduate course in Counseling, which was available, but ...

They suggested, instead, that I take what else was available: a Media Studies programme. '*They*' here was not even someone who knew the first thing about career options. She was just a helpful clerk in the admissions department whose reason for discouraging Counseling was that most people switched courses a few semesters after commencement. It made sense to me then – what doesn't for a purposeless loser?

Somehow I had a feeling I was going to end up helping people, which had prompted my first choice of a study course. I used that as justification for doing exactly what I had done a decade earlier. I settled for what was available.

Like many losers I did not know that patience also has speed. It is always worth waiting for what you really want than to take something you never planned for in the first place. I mean, what if it was a spouse and you married the wrong person? It can be worse with a career.

My last stroke in this series of stupidity was just before I started writing this book. Two years after completing my college degree I migrated to a neighbouring country where a friend was interested in my services as a journalist.

He enticed me with a list of promises. The offer was too lucrative to turn down. Again you guessed right. The usual motivation from the fear of losing the only option available played a great part. I gladly joined him and was to spend a whole two years of empty promises and unappreciated service.

I have never come across an employer so adept at backtracking on his promises. And yet I stayed on, getting what was made available to me. I was very angry and frustrated but never did anything about it. Not even expressing my displeasure to my employer.

I comforted myself by talking *about* my employer to others than confronting and talking *to* him – a common trait with all losers.

Losers cannot stand offending even those who take them for granted. They bear any nonsense quietly, never voicing their displeasure but preferring, instead, to bottle everything in until it boils over, or shoot their mouths in the wrong places.

Losers can even accept a raw deal knowingly and spend the rest of the deal's life whining about unfairness and playing the helpless victim. I was a classic example and it was not just limited to my career.

I could buy the wrong pair of trousers and hate it for as long as I had it. Or I could pick a stale loaf of bread off the shelf and take it home where I would eat it while I cursed the bakery. I could leave the barbershop with a lousy haircut (no complaints whatsoever) and return to the same lousy barber to get messed up again next time; and that list is endless. All because I did not want to challenge anything and, thus, always settled for what was made available instead of insisting for what I wanted.

After using this useless method for many years, I learnt the hard way that you can never achieve anything by accepting whatever is available just because you think there is no option.

Firstly, that is a misleading philosophy. Secondly, there is always an option. A viable option if you demand for it. And you should always insist on the very best possible, not just the best available.

I like a very exciting scene in the 1978 motion picture, *The Wild Geese.* Upon being asked why he had not asked about his payment for the job they had just discussed, Colonel Faulkner promptly responded.

"Well first of all I have to find out if the project is feasible. If it is I will send you the contract," said the smart colonel before adding: "I don't discuss fees, I get what I want!"

Many losers think as I once did, that peace is a consequence of playing dumb and going with the tide. I have news for you. Resistance, when it is due, is a highly beneficial thing. Light, sound, movement and heat are all made possible by some degree of resistance. So is progress.

People and the universe will always stand in your way by resisting all your ideas, efforts and dreams. You will have to resist their indifference in turn to prevail against them and make a difference. Chances are you will have to resist or push twice as much or more.

Survival, the minimum basic requirement of existence, is struggle. And struggle implies resistance. If you do not understand or are comfortable with anything, resist it. You must agree with or accept something because, and only because, you understand and like it.

And in closing this chapter, here is what I have learnt about peace, which is often mistaken for absence of struggle.

Peace can never be achieved by bottling up your concerns just so you can spare the other party some trouble. Peace is a consequence of the confrontation of our problems, situations and the people we deal with when they are not treating us right.

It is a result of your ability to boldly say, 'No! I cannot agree to this until I get what I desire.' It is better to wait than to get less and be shortchanged. If anyone thinks you can take anything they offer you, despite your expectations, then they do not deserve your service, partnership or even attention.

Never deal with anyone who has nothing to lose from your prospective partnership.

And lastly, I was wrong all my life to assume that I have no choice and always had to take what was offered. The truth is that the universe is always abounding with options and YOU carry around all your options to negotiate the best possible deals. Once you settle for less, it is difficult to convince the other party that you can be worth a penny more.

Barclays Bank used to run an intriguing commercial I will never forget. It ended with the tagline: "Get it right the first time!" I learnt this the hard way, but you can learn from my mistake.

Remember getting it right only happens when you decide beforehand what you are worth, how much of that you are willing to compromise and for what benefit, in the immediate or medium term.

Except losers have a hard time making decisions.

Chapter 5

Losers always avoid making decisions

Never avoid making decisions

Learn to make sound decisions all the time

*Whatever the situation, whatever the outcome –
please make a decision*

*If you do not make a decision, one will be made
for you!*

If you can't decide, you won't act

One time as I walked past a gift shop, I saw in the display
window a plaque with the following message:

*"Maturity is the ability to make a decision and
stand by it. The immature people spend all their lives
exploring endless possibilities, then: do nothing."*

This was during my college days. I had no inkling how the immaturity of avoiding making decisions had, and would continue putting my life on hold for a long time.

There are two types of decisions we make. We make conscious and unconscious decisions. Or if you like, deliberate or by default. It is simple really. Either you make a decision deliberately, or you do not. When you decide not to – a decision is automatically taken for you: by YOU!

By way of example; if you are in a lousy place or have accepted a bad deal – life is full of these – and you fail to make a decision to get out, you have just made an even bigger decision: to stay and put up with the crap that will cramp your style and mock every effort you make.

I think that is why Napoleon Hill insisted that: "By any means you must make a decision." Even a bad decision is better than no decision at all.

And if there is something the Universe is super-efficient at, it is making a decision for you when you snooze, second guess or refuse to decide.

Story of my life!

Remember after high school when I did not post back the apprenticeship form? I made a decision to condemn myself to some lowly occupation a few months later.

Being unemployed for a while, I had grown quite comfortable getting out of bed when the sun was up and doing nothing for the rest of the day. Realising this was not working for everyone, my father made a decision for me. He arranged for me a temporary job as a school teacher which lasted three months.

After that I went to college where I failed to say, "No," to a course other than the one I had applied for. A decision was made for me to train as a secretary.

For six months after college I trudged the city of Harare daily in search for work as a secretary, without any break. I was frustrated and desperate. Then one day a consultant candidly told me:

"I have to be honest with you. I have been in this industry for a long time and have placed no more than five male personal assistants. It might take a while before I can place you and you may want to consider chasing something different."

She was making a decision for me and I took her advice and gave up my job search.

A few weeks later I met a friend who said he could get me a job as a clerk in the Social Services department. A month later I was working in some refugee camp as an administration clerk responsible for logistics. A decision had been made for me.

Two years later I was still a clerk because I had made no decision to change my condition. A very close friend I worked with then, made a decision to further his studies. He applied for and was admitted into the school of social work for a four year college diploma. I remained behind wallowing in my indecision.

When the refugee program concluded, my old friend who had invited me to my previous job had joined the insurance industry. After learning that I was struggling in between jobs, he suggested I send my résumé to his company. That is how I became an insurance broker and met a very exciting chap called Mike Mudimu.

Mike was not academically gifted. He barely made it in secondary school, scratching only a couple of subject passes where the minimum requirement for the job market or further studies, was five. But Mike had learnt the significance of making decisions.

And his decision resonates with the wisdom of Professor Albert Einstein:

"Everyone is a genius. But if you judge a fish by its ability to climb a tree, it will live its whole life believing that it is stupid."

Somehow, Mike knew that he was a fish and had no business trying to climb trees. He had decided that he was going to be rich instead. He instantly put school behind him and became an insurance salesman, while others gave their failed exams a second and third chance.

So as soon as Mike had understood and mastered the essentials of the industry he made a decision to leave for a neighbouring country to pursue his dream of becoming financially independent.

It is amazing how I, then Mike's best friend and protégé, was instrumental in his migration. In fact I literally pushed him to apply for a situation I had noticed in a local newspaper for insurance agents in Botswana.

I, personally, made the call to the prospective employer, pretending I was Mike, and all he had to do was go for the interview. He made a decision and the rest is history.

A few years later he was running his own insurance agency successfully while I was stuck in a receptionist's job. He even suggested that I join him and that opportunity was also lost to indecision.

Quite often indecision cost me big time and when I said it was the story of my life I was not exaggerating. I am the guy you would see walk into a shop, try out some jeans but fail to make a decision to buy. Yes even when they fit perfectly and I have the money in my pocket to spend on clothing. Somehow when the time is right I would just lapse into indecision.

It seems that as soon as I had all the information and resources needed to make a decision; I would become uncertain what to do next.

At one time, after meeting with that transformational expert who prompted me to conceive some purpose for my existence, I resolved to become a change agent. I had one major aim in mind: to ensure that no person I could influence can ever grow up to become 34 without a well-defined vision or purpose as I had done.

I conceived and worked on a five module personal development programme which I sent to my old friends on three continents for review and send feedback. All of them were very excited about the project and readily told me it was great and needed to be launched immediately. Indecision hit again and the project was put on hold indefinitely.

You see, the immediate product of indecision is what Paul Myers calls; *the biggest non-informational hurdle to success* that most of us face – "The failure to take action."

If you cannot decide you cannot act. But, guess what? Still things happen around you. The universe never waits for the undecided.

Invariably, everything you will ever need in this short life is safely tucked beneath action. But you must first decide to act.

By any means, make a decision today and start changing your life!

Chapter 6:

Losers Are Ill-Disciplined

Indiscipline is a form of laziness
Nothing ever gets done without discipline
Do not mistake activity for productivity

Almost always, the biggest common denominator in all losers is lack of discipline – self-discipline to be precise. Indeed, whichever way you look at anything, nothing ever gets done without discipline.

I will say that again: NOTHING EVER GETS ACCOMPLISHED WITHOUT DISCIPLINE!

Discipline is the decision to take action in discharging what must be done regardless of your emotional state. Indiscipline, on the other hand, is choosing to do the easier thing (that you do not really have to do) because it is more pleasurable than what you must do. Does that sound familiar?

How many times have you chosen to watch truckloads of television, instead of reading a good book, rehearsing a sales pitch or working on an assignment from school or work?

Ever noticed how it is convenient to do this or spend hours chatting on social networks instead of doing homework, making sales calls, balancing your books or doing what puts bread on your table and pays for that Internet facility.

Indiscipline is an active form of laziness. It generates action without results - in short, *activity*; while discipline creates action with results, i.e. *productivity*.

Losers specialize in activity while winners or successful people focus on productivity. The funny thing is that when you walk into a room where both losers and winners are supposed to be doing some work – everyone will be looking busy – losers often look even busier than the winners. They have mastered the *art of looking busy*. A lot of people actually get paid for this in many work places!

Before we go into my experience with indiscipline let me make a few things clear about discipline.

Discipline implies action, hard work, focus,

consistency and honesty. All these success traits are what translate into integrity. You cannot fake any one of them and all have no substitutes. I spent over two decades trying to fake and/or substitute them with no success at all.

I was a lazy person and always thought being *clever* (I am sure you know the difference between clever and smart) would make up for that. I created a shortcut or an effortless way for doing almost everything that required action, hard work and focus.

As early as primary school, I developed a skill for tuning in to what the teacher would say during lessons and made sure I remembered it to the exam day. That way I never had to read after lessons or wake up early in the morning to study before going to school. Even for examinations. Sleeping and waking up late were celebrated habits.

In secondary school I elevated my laziness to cramming and identifying main lesson concepts and recording them in the most summarized phrases in a few notebooks. Where others had a dozen notebooks, I had only one or two which I could scan through on the morning of an exam and emerge from the examination room afterward smiling from ear to ear.

I complemented that with ensuring I joined every discussion group I came across. To eliminate further odds, I made it a consistent habit to collect past exam papers and studied their trend such that I could tell with more than 80% accuracy what was likely to come in a particular examination.

It was a special way of cheating which needed very little effort and time and paid off during the rest of my formal schooling experience. All the time created from these shenanigans, I redirected to uselessness: hanging around with girls, reading novels, idle chattering, playing excessive chess and sleeping till the sun was up.

So I passed all my exams and never once failed a public exam up to college. I literally succeeded in beating the system for as long as I remained in school. I was to learn later that in the practical world, life was not about beating the exam system. And that you cannot cram your way through to harvesting time on the farm.

In real life you reap what you sow; after painstakingly nourishing the shoot with sweat, blood and tears and patiently waiting for it till harvest time. There are no shortcuts or substitutes – except when you decide to buy plastic flowers, plastic fruits and plastic trees, which do not smell at all, neither are they of any use when you become hungry.

It is worth recounting here a small snag to my chicanery and how laziness once buried me for a while.

Among the subject mixes at both secondary school and college were some that were known as 'practical' subjects and required regular practice. They included mathematics and accounts.

Realizing the only way to *cheat* through mathematics was regular practice I resolved to drop the subject from my list and squandered the exam fee. Later this seriously handicapped my options whenever an opening for anything that required mathematics came up. It was the reason I could not take either business studies or marketing management in college and ended up settling for secretarial studies. The chickens had come back home to roost.

Take it from me; life always comes full circle.

In college I struggled with accounts which needed regular practice. All the time I had for practice I devoted to playing chess, my girlfriend, television and drinking.

So I resorted to copying others' work before submission for marking and often came highest because

I had the time to compare answers from my classmates' assignments and write down the common ones. I made a lot of fun out of this and no one was really bothered about my habit. Instead they named me 'Copy Accountant.' A few guys ended up submitting their assignments at my dorm room the night before so that I could conveniently copy their work and then submit all the books to the lecturer the following morning.

Two weeks before the final exam, my roommate – a figures whiz – let me in on a few secrets about accounting. And since most of the marks had accumulated from the year's coursework – the bulk of which I had copied from others – the rest was a piece of cake.

I was pretty disappointed to discover that in the real world there was no coursework and you cannot wait to copy another person's work without getting fired first.

It is worse with those who sleep their way through examinations, job interviews and up the corporate ladder. The problem is that one can never cheat hard work indefinitely without complications; often sooner than later.

Other than cheating I learnt and mastered the art of, what Dr Schwartz calls, *excusitis* and perfectionism to delay action indefinitely.

Many things I never achieved in my first forty years of existence – which I should have – were actually never started in the first place. I can list tens of my brilliant ideas that never saw the light of the day.

Dr. Myles Munroe once said if you want to get great ideas that have never been tried; the place to look for them is the graveyard. Many losers carry around life-altering ideas without once attempting to transmute them into action, until they die.

While in secondary school, I always wanted to write a novel and had a few good stories with great plots and story lines – courtesy of the hundreds of novels I had read and an adventurous high school *love* life. All of them were miscarried before their birth. I just could not get started. Every time it looked like I was going to start, I always found something easier to preoccupy me, like another novel to read.

Evidently it was way easier and more exciting to read what somebody else had written than to write my own story for others to read. This is how subtle indiscipline can become. Reading is great, but when it becomes an excuse for not writing your own work, it deteriorates into *activity* instead of productivity.

I tried the same thing in college with the same abortive result, and later after college – and yes, with nothing produced for consumption still. My excuse was that there were far too many people writing novels and mine was not likely to make any difference or excite any attention. A possible career as a novelist went begging.

When I eventually got to write something it was on personal development. Over three years of putting together ideas, concepts and experiences resulted in many long sleepless nights of developing power point slides and then modules. At the time of writing this book I had five finished modules. Five complete soft copy manuscripts that were undergoing perfectionism. Another sexy form of indiscipline.

I needed to start and finish something before I turned 40. That inspired my dogged determination to complete this book in less than two months.

It was not a stroll in the park. Getting started was a challenge. And when, at last, I got round to doing something, remaining focused was a big pain in the neck. Distractions were available wholesale.

A colleague at work was downloading latest

movies at the rate of three daily and making sure I got them at the end of each day.

On the other hand, every time I logged on to the internet I was inundated by Facebook updates, links to music sites – I love music and can spend hours on end sampling and downloading tracks. And then there was unsolicited mail in my inboxes. I had three different e-mail addresses and all of them received tons of mail on the hour.

Then there were a constant influx of telephone calls and SMSs to ensure nothing resembling concentration or focus ever obtained.

Being a loser I always tried to attend to every single of these urgent but not important things. It was not surprising that I could accomplish literally nothing of my own despite getting into the office as early as 6am and leaving around 11pm. Yes, 14 to 17 hours later, exhausted but with nothing to show for all that time investment. Activity without productivity, or put simply - indiscipline.

Again, I learnt the painful way that discipline implies deciding what to do and focus on just that, even if it means you block all unnecessary calls, attend to e-mails only at certain times – and even then, after ruthlessly screening them. It meant just smiling at unimportant SMSs that are ironically never short at all and often encrypted in some terrible *shorthand* that is so painful to decipher.

Take for example this useless gibberish for an SMS: *"hi, js 2 sei, hw u dng. m gr8. bn ages n js thot I shd chck on u. v a gr8 dei."* And no it is not German!

When I resolved to be organized, I watched movies during weekends as a bonus for getting something important done during the week. I allocated a few hours to YouTubing, downloading music and other miscellaneous files from the endless torrents on the internet.

And then there was peer pressure but I will spare you details on this daily evil. Just remember that the best way to deal with peer pressure is to know when to politely but boldly say "No thanks." Nothing is more empowering and more solid a foundation for building self-discipline, than to cultivate the habit of saying, "no" as often as you can.

Next to peer pressure was the pressure to please others; even strangers I had just met and would probably never remember me a few minutes after we had parted ways.

It took me a very long time to realize that people will always get wherever they intend to go and accomplish whatever they intended to do, with or, without my assistance. I also learnt that I should never feel obliged to help everyone – a seemingly great but overzealous pursuit that is not sustainable in the long run. You simply cannot help everyone. You only get ahead as you learn to know how far you can go in helping others.

Lastly, my indiscipline took the form of procrastination. This is a kind of insanity where I started assuming that I will live forever on God's Ever Green Earth. I even became convinced that tomorrow would always be fine and longer than today. Long enough to absorb both its obligations and some leftovers from today. How easy it was for me to say: "I will pick it up from here tomorrow."

Once that became routine, nothing ever got finished and every tomorrow became more shrunken and congested. I had no idea where to start. While I was at it, indecision would take over and then inaction.

And in case you start getting any clever ideas, be warned. In real life there is neither fast forward nor rewind except in your head. So, when you find yourself in a rut, stop digging and decide what to sacrifice in order to un-mess your situation.

For sacrifice, options are endless. They range over: sleep, friends, television, social outings, clubbing, prattle and idling that have now assumed the form of incessant internet chat on Facebook, G-talk, Whatsapp, Tweeter, Skype, Instagram and others.

Social outings, clubbing and idling on the social networks must be your first casualties. Meanwhile, a big slice from each of the others will give you a lot of time and energy to salvage your mess and catch up.

It is simply an act of balancing the equation and in the real world nothing goes unaccounted for or without severe consequences.

I have remarkably made some strides in the area of discipline. I finished writing the first draft of this particular chapter at exactly 2.42am on a Wednesday morning and the next day started in exactly 3 hours and 18 minutes.

Here is a smart way of reorganising your social life doing something worthwhile, while having a blast and getting better. For social outings, join any active citizenship club like; JCI (Junior Chamber International), Toastmasters International, Lions Club International, or Red Cross International. If you are younger, you can join the Scouts or Junior Achiever.

In these clubs you meet very progressive people, who are focused and have lots of knowledge and skills to share. You will also get to learn very useful leadership and related skills that you can use at work and in business. They are also a great networking platform. But most importantly, you will get the opportunity to do something fulfilling through voluntary contribution or active citizenship.

And while you think of who you are hanging around a lot, remember you are the average of the five people you spend the most time with.

Time to have a closer look at the company you are regularly keeping. You may need to let some of them go, for your progress!

Chapter 7

Losers never finish anything they start

> *Waste no time in getting started*
>
> *Stick with it to the end*
>
> *Persist until you accomplish what you set out to do*
>
> *Finish everything you start*
>
> *Refuse to do anything else until you finish the task at hand*

Losers specialize in building foundations.

One of the major reasons I decided to write this book was because I had to start something that I really needed to finish and put a stop to my loser's streak. I told myself that I had to finish this one project on my own without chasing any exam or work deadline. I resolved that the draft manuscript had to be ready in exactly 60 days or less.

Before that I never got to complete anything of my own and if all my initiatives were like meals, I shudder to imagine how the long queue of partly touched plates would have looked like behind me.

You probably might have come across Ed Frank's remark:

"*I think* there are two types of people in this world – people who can start things and people who can finish things."

A long time ago I took this observation in an ill-informed way and used it to justify not being able to complete everything important I ever started. I decided I was a good starter but a lousy finisher. This is the most idiotic theory I ever invented for my indiscipline, lack of focus and inability to persevere until succeeding. Or at least just finish something notable.

While I was struggling to finish this book, I had five modules on personal development pending. Not only that, I was supposed to register a company for me to be able to commercialize or, at least, render my programmes recognizable by the respective authorities.

That never happened and a lot of opportunities where squandered. But then, remember losers live as if they are here forever.

Back in my late twenties I remember starting a youth religious organisation and despite having a lot of support from the local business community, I just left it to fizzle into nothing after a year before it died a quiet natural death.

I started yet another one some years later and it died at constitution writing level.

Just before I had started writing this book, I had resolved that I was going to do two major things before I hit 40.

First I wanted to launch a lifestyle magazine and then use it to start a not-for profit venture where I would set up high tech learning centres in rural areas to help the children there catch up on and compete with the rest of the world using modern technologies. I prepared two great documents articulating the ideas underlying these projects, identified possible partners and even ran the idea past some of them for buy in.

They were all sold in to the idea and very eager to get started. Then the usual happened. Everything was put on hold and joined a terrifying queue of unfinished business. And all this has absolutely nothing to do with the world being peopled by either starters or finishers.

If it was not plain laziness, it was loss of focus or sliding back into the comfort zone, where I have spent all my life wallowing in mediocrity while others pressed ahead.

I could have heeded one of Og Mandino's powerful declarations:

"I will persist until I succeed."

You may want to say that too: "I will persist until I succeed!" And that is the magic formula to success.

But I never heeded and always started many other things before finishing any of the projects at hand first. The result was split attention, loss of energy and, eventually, inaction. I degenerated into a serial starter who never finished anything.

As I mentioned before, my other weakness was perfectionism.

I always wanted things to come out perfect, with the result that most of the time they died while undergoing perfectionism. Remember that delaying anything makes it even scarier and bigger every day that passes. All the things that you put off will surely balloon out of size before you and scare you from acting. Meanwhile opportunities do not wait for people who specialize in snoozing. You snooze you lose.

The other thing is that I never took anything important seriously for long, assuming that delay would eventually render them unnecessary.

But perhaps one of the biggest sins and injustices to myself and a few other people that really counted on me, was my inability to stand up to those who took advantage of me.

This brings us to the next evil trait of losers...

Chapter 8

Losers take crap while sitting

Learn and practice voicing your concern

Boldly speak out against any form of abuse

Confront your problems – speak to them and not about them

If need be, play hardball to get what you deserve

Yes! Losers take crap with no questions asked.

A loser will take any sort of nonsense dumped on his or her lap by anyone, who cares to, without a word. Fear debilitates a loser from voicing against injustice, ill-treatment and abuse; be it in an intimate relationship, friendship, at work, or even in a supermarket queue.

Anybody will make a doormat of someone who is not willing to stand up and protest. And the beauty of it all is that we give people clues on how to treat us. Or to use Miguel Ruiz's words, we use others as an excuse to abuse ourselves.

My life has been pretty much this kind of nonsense and I have quietly taken truckloads of crap for longer than I can remember – no questions asked.

At first I would resort to running away quietly. Almost all of my previous job movements were inspired by flight – but as I grew older I discovered I could not run forever. Yet instead of standing up to my challenges and confronting people and situations that needed to hear my piece of mind, often times, I would expend a lot of energy bitching about my boss, my wife, my colleagues (even subordinates) or anyone I could not face – which was almost everyone – behind their backs.

That is all I ever did for as long as I remained a receptionist for seven drab years at a company that was so big it had many situations I could take advantage of and migrate from my parroting job. I knew there were opportunities for me elsewhere in other departments but I never once approached the human resource department to make a staff movement request.

For seven years I preferred to assume that HR knew I wanted to move. When they did nothing, which was highly likely because they thought I was comfortable where I was, I started thinking someone did not care about my career development.

I resorted to complaining to the wrong people in the wrong quarters, with the obvious results. I even have a feeling my malicious sentiments reached my boss' ears and he, in turn, quietly resented me and made sure I remained where I was – in a rut. By the way the only difference between a rut and a grave is that a rut is shallower.

At one point after reading *Fire and Water*, a book co-authored by Reg Lescaris and Mike Lipkin, I just felt so provoked and tendered in my resignation to the human resource department the following morning.

They were reluctant to let me go. When they enquired what the problem was, I told them:

"Someone offered me a better job with a better salary."

They simply counter offered the salary but said nothing about a better job. Neither did I.

I took the new salary, which was probably overdue, and went back to my useless job. An opportunity to play hardball and change workstations went down the drain kicking and screaming. A few months down the line the feeling of dissatisfaction crept back in, and with it the rotten habit of whining in the wrong places and to the wrong people.

Not only is this a shameful trait, but one that often makes the problem even bigger, especially if those you dishonour during their absence get wind of it.

Always be loyal to the absent.

We have to be clear about two things at this point.

Firstly, the lowly and contemptuous habit of backbiting includes any negative talk about someone during their absence, whether what you talk about is true or not.

Secondly, backbiting is a form of cowardice that nurtures the corrosive form of fear called resentment in you the backbiter. Someone has aptly described resentment as drinking poison and expecting someone else to die. Dr. Bobbe Sommer calls it anger gone rotten.

The habit of speaking ill of others behind their backs, often characterized by scandal mongering to make it more sensational to the listener – and often to someone who cannot do anything to help you or your situation – is a vocation for many losers. It is an unpaid occupation that squanders lots of time and energy.

Most losers use this habit to trash others in the hope of getting ahead. But life often comes full circle and when it does you get to appreciate the old adage:

"Always make sure that your words are sweet and soft because you may, have to eat them back."

Quite often, sooner than later!

I will always admire my best friend and college roommate. I have always tried, with no success, to recall one moment when John ever got to dishonour anyone absent. He maintained this very illustrious character for the two full academic years we shared a college dorm room.

His secret, as I discovered in my reflective and soul searching excursions later, was that John would rather talk *to,* than talk *about* anyone who annoyed him. Little wonder everyone sincerely respected him and found it easy to confide in him the most profound of personal matters.

Many years later, after feeding the counterproductive habit of dishonouring the absent and creating more problems for myself, I felt depression and stress weighing me down and could not help recalling how John was always the spirit of any party back in college.

I also discovered that his attitude was both an indispensable personal and leadership quality with which challenges and tricky situations can be effectively dealt at all times.

I have particularly singled out this weakness (bitching about in the wrong places) because many losers find it the easiest way out of their problems when they are afraid to confront people who treat them unfairly. Unfortunately it is a gateway to a dead end a 100% of the time.

Any tricky or sticky situation in life often inspires two possible reactions: fight or flight. If you must ever amount to anything worthwhile, make sure to always dig your heels in and fight. Every human being is born with some amazing amount of fight in them that can only be realized by tapping it every time the situation demands.

But two things deplete that fight: taking nonsense quietly and then slandering your imagined adversary behind their back. Both are useless ways of avoiding confrontation. Yet confrontation is both good and healthy, especially if it is all for noble intentions. Sometimes it is a bit uncomfortable, but in the end it certainly pays off. A lot of time and energy is saved in the process and people get to respect and treat you accordingly.

Remember the words of Mariane Williamson:

"Your playing small does not serve the world. There is nothing enlightened about shrinking so that other people won't feel insecure around you."

Cut yourself some slack: stand up and say something, or simply raise your head high from wherever you are and boldly say 'No!' to nonsense or rubbish. You are not a trashcan and anyone holding their crap before you should take it elsewhere.

I allowed myself to be a doormat for the best part of my life's first 40 years, and through this shameful experience realized that it is definitely a disgraceful trait not even worthy of a dog. But it is something you can turn around and deal with decisively.

You start by making a conscious decision that you will not brook any nonsense from anyone, even if they were breathing real fire from seven heads and standing on a dozen giant legs. Let the dragon eat you up first before you entertain any nonsense from it without voicing your concern.

You, like David and Samson, have no business accepting any *hot air* even if it is from something that looks as fierce as Goliath or as formidable as the Philistines army. And today we have better weapons than a sling and an ass' jaw bone. It is called freedom of expression or knowledge.

Stand up against nonsense and earn yourself some respect.

A scene in the movie, *The Aviator* illustrates what I am saying in a very intriguing way. Pissed off by Senator Brewster's crap, during one of the senate hearings, Howard Hughes grabs the microphone and defiantly declares:

> "Now I am supposed to be many things which are not complimentary. I am supposed to be capricious, I have been called a playboy, I have even been called an eccentric but I do not believe that I have the reputation of being a liar...

> "Now Senator Brewster, you can subpoena me, you can arrest me, you can even claim that I folded up and taken a run ... but ... well, I have had just enough of this nonsense.

> "Good afternoon!"

And out strolled Howard Hughes in a move that buried his adversary.

Jim Rohn used to call this: "The Day That Changed Your Life." or the "I have had it!" moment.

It happens when you allow yourself to be annoyed enough to tell anyone off in their face. Nothing can be more liberating!

Chapter 9

Losers are just plain lazy

Get off your butt and do something

There is no nobility in avoiding work,

And

Nothing ever gets achieved without hard work

Losers avoid anything that puts them under pressure, or the heat of the moment, to get what has to be done out of the way. They have no clue that anything of value has had to be subjected to extraordinary amounts of pressure, heat and slamming; over long periods, to become valuable.

Coal, steel, diamonds and gold were all, valueless dirt a long time ago and had to be subjected to high temperatures, pressure and passage of time in order to achieve value. It is the same with human beings.

Nothing gets achieved without 'doing.' Just *being* is not enough; you have to be a *humandoing* most of the time or when action calls. Talk is cheap and convenient. Only action makes the desired difference.

I have always wondered what it would take to earn the kind of money that Oprah Winfrey, Will Smith, Usain Bolt, Floyd Mayweather Jr and Jay Z rack in every year, and I discovered one common trait that gave life to all their successful pursuits.

They work very hard!

Yes, there are no other secrets. Dogged slogging that has no respect, whatsoever, for fatigue; defies any form of excusitis; is not bound by traditional timelines and their socially crafted meanings; regards sleep a non-profitable luxury and is inspired by the quest to be done, only when the work is done. Before that, nothing else but the task at hand matters.

All high net worth people work harder than you can start to imagine. Artists and sportspeople spend longer than 18 hours in the studio and many hours in the gym pumping tones of weights and making hundreds of choreographed dance moves.

They voraciously devour literature. Why do you think they are always quoting from all these endless books on their shows and in their interviews? They learn everything there is to learn in order to get ahead of times and remain relevant in a super dynamic world where the only constant thing is change.

Research has shown that average CEOs read at least 60 books a year. That is, five books a month! I am sure you know what CEOs do for a living?

I love the way musician and entrepreneur Lil Wayne puts it:

"I try not to sleep."

How is that for a work ethic?

Success comes as a result of burning the midnight oil, busting one's backside and seeing to it that the task at hand is effectively dispensed with.

Working hard is not a gift you are born with. It is a decision you make on your own. But since losers are bad decision makers, most just do not ever get around to making the decision to work hard at any stage in their lives. Yes even if their life depended on it! And it always does.

The snooze button on the wake-up alarm devices

was made with the loser in mind. I had a friend who used to tell me that he hits the snooze button on his alarm watch no less than twice every morning. What he did not know, because I did not tell him, was that my alarm was set at 5 minute snooze intervals and my daily morning snoozing routine carried on for a whole hour!

In this way and many others, for over 30 years, I worked very hard to become a loser. Every loser does.

I avoided hard work. I always reported sick on any day of strenuous work, or endeared myself to prefects (in school) or supervisors (at work) so I could always get the lighter tasks. That usually included a fair amount of sucking up to those in authority.

All these ugly tricks are not sustainable in the long run, and it took me a good part of my first forty years to discover this.

Today there are endless preoccupations on the Internet to make you look like you are doing something, when you are actually skiving.

You can *facebook* until the cows come home, *g-talk* all the prattle there is in the wretched world, *YouTube* every song or video clip you can spell, invest unbelievably long hours consuming x-rated material on porn sites or just following gossip on the tens of tabloids that churn out negative and depressing stuff wholesale by the minute. But you will get nowhere notable in life.

If you do not bust your backside now, sooner than later, you will go bust yourself. Success is spelt: H.A.R.D.W.O.R.K! The only thing you achieve without hard work is poverty and misery. There is plenty of that around already, it no longer looks fashionable!

Ask yourself now:

Am I working hard enough to float above poverty now and wretchedness in future?

When he or she appears, the lazy loser is very easy to recognise. He or she has a lot of hot air coming from every opening on his or her body – especially the mouth – and nothing tangible to show for it. Chances are also very high that he or she *knows everything* there is to know.

The other version of a loser simply dissolves into the crowd somewhere unnoticeable and concentrates on being invisible.

I have done both for long but with very little success. Learn from me; you sure do not have to go through this yourself. Not too many people ever get to write books about this!

The only reason I ever got to publish this book is because I had resolved to work as hard as I had never done before. The prospects, if I can call them that, of dying a loser, were so ghastly to me they excited goose bumps all over my body and inside my head.

Chapter 10

Losers are spineless

It's not all about talent

It's not all about education

It's not even about genius

It's about guts

Take a leap of faith, jump off the cliff and learn to fly on the way down!

Success in life is really about guts. I do not know of anything that was ever achieved without the aid of some serious guts.

My former university lecturer and great friend, Webster Muonwa always argued that guts were the reason most less intelligent and not so talented people he has come across ever became successful. Not talent, education or intellectual endowment.

"The world," said Calvin Coolidge, "is full of unsuccessful people with talent, educated derelicts and unrewarded genius."

Just look around you and count the amazing number of talented alcoholics busy becoming nothing notable. It is because many of these people lack the guts to try the next tricky thing, swim in uncharted waters or get out their comfort zone.

I was an above average student all my school years and if I had put my mind to it, I would have excelled to the top of the heap. I discovered my talent in primary school. I read a lot and wrote very exciting stories in class. I made my very first public speech presentation at a religious congregation well before I was in third grade.

I was a great dancer and a valuable one too. Remember the day I jumped on stage during a live performance and won myself $5.00 for my two minute antics.

In high school, all my talents were even amplified.

I was the senior reporter for the school sports newsletter, best member in the first winning English language debating club at my school and the best student from the creative writing club. I was a big hit.

But I lacked guts and when it really mattered I froze and watched, in amazement. Meanwhile the mediocre around me completely transformed their fortunes by jumping for opportunities while I was busy trying to process my possible success rate against imagined risks. I was a very creative person. But I obviously did a good job of manufacturing viable, so to speak, reasons why I would fail if I ever tried.

And this is a disease that traced its origins to when I was just a small boy.

In the first grade, I developed an intense crush for a very beautiful girl in my class called Margaret and I had a feeling she liked me too. We played together a lot, we spoke a lot and I visited her at her parents' shop where I would get some snacks and change for movies. But I never summoned enough guts to tell her how I felt about her. Of course I was seven, but then so what.

Soon after the second grade Maggie moved towns to live with her older brother. This left me so heartbroken. I never stopped thinking about her for several months and it took me the rest of grade school to get over her and move on with my life. All I ever needed to do was write the words, 'I love you!' on a small piece of paper and hand it over to her. It never happened.

My late bosom friend, some crazy but smart kid, cajoled me many times to tell Maggie but he might as well have been trying to trap a flooding river using his tiny hands.

One time he almost killed me with shock when he threatened to go and tell Maggie that I had a soft spot for her. I remember vividly how I begged with him and later threatened to sever our friendship if he did. I think the threat came out very convincingly because little Wally took it seriously and backed off. Many years later I wished he had called my bluff.

I met Maggie 12 years later when we were both college students and guts failed me again. I had all the leverage I needed but I still felt I needed something more. God knows what.

I broke the news to her on *facebook* just before I turned 40 and now, over 30 years later, it really made no difference if she knew or not. We both laughed it out loud and went back to more pressing nonsense in our immediate situations.

I have had numerous instances where I would have made it big time, if only I had taken a leap. But everything always fell through at the point where life required me to walk off the edge and dive into the unknown. Faced with this option I have always lapsed into a trance and let openings go begging while I explored endless possibilities that never crystalised into anything resolute.

I lacked guts to say, "Yes," when anything life altering came my way. I failed to grab opportunities that happened by my neighbourhood and to say "no," to circumstances that disadvantaged me. Instead of walking away from useless environments and relationships, I have had to remain stuck in degrading situations and their deception of security.

I have put up with abusive people because I was afraid that a change in the nature of the relationship might be worse than the pain of the abuse.

It is hard to imagine a more screwed up life.

Like many fellow gutless losers, I ended up taking recourse to the most common contemptible options for not stepping off the cliff. They include:

1. Waiting for someone to notice me – very tricky because everybody is busy with their own thing. And even when they get a breather, there are far too many gutless losers waiting to be spotted and it is almost always not you

2. Backtracking – and then creating some mollifying excuse for not taking the plunge. The thing is, those who will ever listen to your chicken little story do not really give a damn and it does not give you any mileage. And, by the way, people without guts always have a fallback plan. They will always need something to fall back on, often something with lesser risk and, therefore, of lesser or no value as well.

3. Minding Other People's Business – a paradise for the gutless. In this vocation, you jump every day, but you never have to jump off the edge. It is literally jumping all over the place for all the wrong reasons and intents: other people's reasons and intents!

4. Becoming a Philosopher – here, one gradually deteriorates into a philosopher with all the answers to why the fall from the cliff will result into certain death at the foot of the mountain. Or, worse still, the stupid reasoning that the fall might be an eternal one into a bottomless pit with no prospects of ever landing. Anything to scare the wits out of a person so they can refrain from taking the leap.

5. Refusing to Get Fed Up – and what mischievous use of resilience this turns out to be.

Common with the gutless in this category is the expression: "This time I am fed up," or the classic, "I am sick and tired of ...." After that, they still go back and sit on the receiving end of others' nonsense. The truth is, almost all gutless losers never get fed up of being fed up. Neither do they ever get sick and tired of being sick and tired. It is their way of life.

6. And eventually, the gutless are wont to resign to fate. What more? Someone should have written or determined that fate. Why do you think they have no desire, whatsoever, to change their approach to life.

For the gutless the timeless adage, "if it is to be, it is up to me," often comes out as, "if is to be it is up to circumstances." Little wonder it is common to hear a loser say: "Providing it doesn't rain," or "If the boss grants me a leave day, or "If my partner gives consent," or the classic; "When the economy improves ..." That list is endless.

There are many reasons for this lack of guts, but they can all be safely summed up under the word, fear. Fear of the unknown, made worse by inaction and the vicious circle – of fear alternated with inaction – takes form.

To break it, all one needs to do is to step aside, look at all the missed opportunities and ask: why did I let all those breaks slip through my fingers?

Answers will include, vain attempts to avoid rejection, loss (even of what you do not have yet!), fear of upsetting a few stupid socially crafted rules (not to be confused with laws); a disempowering ego fed by useless early life experiences, false beliefs; confusing persistence with trouble and poor self-image. The last reason is often carved out of misleading conceptions of other losers and a personal runaway imagination that sees only a bleak future.

The reality is that neither the past nor the future really matter when it comes to making the life changing decision to step off the cliff and court the unchartered territory. Only the present moment – the NOW – matters and your deciding factor must invariably be your gut.

Oh yes Webster my friend; It's guts damn it!

This book could have easily fizzled into one of my aborted 'silly' ideas. Only this time I set out to go against the grain and boy, did it take guts and some brass stuff!

It had to be done.

The Final Chapter

Losers like to play it safe

Be bold and go for the big challenges in life

Court adventure, nothing happens in shallow calm waters

Failing and losing are sure indications you are on course to success

But I always played it safe. This is all I ever did beyond 8 years of age right up to 40. I treaded with extreme caution in everything, always going with the flow, straight down and never against the grain.

That is why I have preferred working for others all my life up to middle age without thinking of starting my own small thing to grow. Remember losers like to mind other people's business instead of starting their own.

In high school I was notorious for being the guy who never got turned down by girls. What everyone did not know was that, *The Scientist*, as they touted me for this false achievement, never asked until he was extremely sure the answer would be an unequivocal YES! Pathetic isn't it?

The truth is that I never took chances and almost always never got, as in the case of my first grade attraction – Maggie, to be with someone I really loved so dearly.

Like every other loser, I played it safe because I dreaded rejection. Losing or failing terrified me like hell. If I thought I would lose or fail, I refrained from trying and that kept me away from many of life's adventures that would have enlivened the drab that my first 40 years of existence turned out to be.

I suppose, I took failure and losing a bit too seriously, and never imagined anything beyond them. That is also why I never flunked a single public examination. It did not matter that I passed; it mattered that I never failed!

On the other hand if I became very good at anything and at some point started losing, my interest would gradually ebb and eventually I would call it quits. That is how I stopped playing chess and abandoned many other pursuits, midway, whenever I started doubting I would make it for long.

Now on the other side of 40, I realize, with much disappointment, how all the breakthroughs in the history of mankind were almost always unexpected results of persistent attempts by men and women who never stopped trying until something gave.

Michael Jordan, the American Basketball Legend and the face of Nike, is number one in NBA history in only one category: *the missed shots!* Jordan missed more shots in his NBA career than anybody else and he celebrates this achievement most.

Jackie Chan makes the best action movies, thanks to the numerous failed stunts that dominate his film making stints.

I found the introduction to the book, "Audacity of Hope," by Barak Obama quite heartbreaking. It is about rejection and how Obama decided to mock this rejection and went on to become the most powerful man of his time, in the world, as the United States President.

Most importantly, it is a lesson to all the losers of this world that failure will not kill you; and what doesn't kill you will make you stronger.

I could recount my whole life in terms of missed opportunities owing to playing it safe, but suffice it to say, this will only give you predictable results – if at all – and predictable results never make any difference in any life circumstance.

In this regard, Henry David Thoreau captured the loser's fate nicely in his remark:

"Most men (and women) lead lives of quiet desperation and go to the grave with the song still in them."

The reason I wrote this book may as well be to ensure that this does not happen to others. Many will, however, argue that we do not learn from stories of failures. I have only one argument to counter that: If you know what does not work you can always avoid it, or at least recognise it earlier enough to confront it with a far better chance of overcoming it.

Life is not a procession of gaiety and it is naïve to eliminate the loser's testimony from our success seminars.

And now let's face it my dear friend. Aren't you glad, that I was a loser for the first forty years of my life?

www.ingramcontent.com/pod-product-compliance
Lightning Source LLC
Chambersburg PA
CBHW070519030426
42337CB00016B/2025